Refuse to Use

A Girl's Guide to Drugs and Alcohol

Ann Kirby-Payne

the rosen publishing group's

rosen central

new york

Thanks to my editor, Erica Smith, whose patience made this project possible and whose giggle made it so fun. Special thanks to my dog, Sally, for keeping my feet warm during late nights in front of the computer, and to my husband, Danyal, for making the coffee strong.

Published in 1999 by The Rosen Publishing Group, Inc.
29 East 21st Street, New York, NY 10010

First Edition

Library of Congress Cataloging-in-Publication Data

Kirby-Payne, Ann.
        Refuse to use : a girl's guide to drugs and alcohol / Ann Kirby-Payne
            p.   cm. — (Girls' guides)
        Includes bibliographical references and index.
        Summary: Discusses reasons why teenage girls, in particular, should avoid taking different drugs and offers advice on health concerns and self-esteem.
        ISBN 0-8239-2982-5
        1. Drug abuse Juvenile literature.   2. Alcoholism Juvenile literature.   3. Girls—Drug use Juvenile Literature.   4. Girls—Alcohol use Juvenile litera-
            ture. [1. Drug abuse.   2. Alcoholism.] I. Title.   II. Series.
    HV5809.5.K57 1999
    362.29'084'22—dc21

                                                                            99-2304
                                                                            CIP

Manufactured in the United States of America

ⒸОntents

About This Book

The middle school years are like a roller coaster—wild and scary but also fun and way cool. One minute you're way, way up there, and the next minute you're plunging down into the depths. Not surprisingly, sometimes you may find yourself feeling confused and lost. Not to worry, though. Just like on a roller-coaster ride, at the end of all this crazy middle school stuff, you'll be laughing and screaming and talking about how awesome it all was.

Right now, however, chances are your body is changing so much that it's barely recognizable, your old friends may not share your interests anymore, and your life at school is suddenly hugely complicated. And let's not even get into the whole boy issue. It's a wonder that you can still think straight at all.

Fortunately, reader dear, help is here. This book is your road map. It's also a treasure chest filled with ideas and advice. Armed with this book and with your own inner strength (trust us, you have plenty), you can safely, confidently navigate the twists and turns of your middle school years. It will be tough going, and sometimes you'll wonder if you'll ever get through it. But you—fabulous, powerful, unique you—are up to the task. This book is just a place to start.

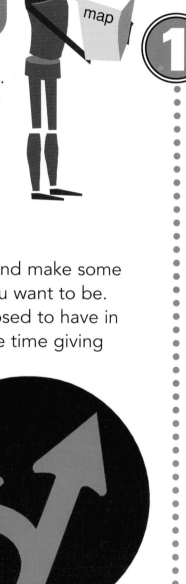

Chart Your Course

1

So you're heading toward adulthood. There are lots of things ahead of you and lots of decisions to make. You and your friends are going through many changes right now, and the road ahead is full of twists and turns that can be confusing, exciting, and scary all at the same time.

It's time to grow up, girlfriend, and make some tough, smart decisions about who you want to be. You can have all the fun you're supposed to have in your teenage years, while at the same time giving yourself the respect you deserve (and earning the respect of everyone around you). Or you can go blindly out onto the road to adulthood and probably wind up getting lost. It's totally up to you.

It's a Woman Thing

It's not easy being female, no matter how old you are and no matter where you live. Girls and women have to deal with certain expectations, prejudices, and realities that boys and men will never really understand. And some things are especially dangerous for women.

Although drug use and abuse are widespread among both males and females of all ages, women who abuse drugs face different risks than do men. Drugs from nicotine to cocaine have been linked to various forms of cancer in women. Drugs lessen your chances of having a healthy baby someday, and some can cause horrible birth defects if you take them while you're pregnant. Even if you are not pregnant, taking some drugs can affect your chances of ever having children.

And if you think it ends there, think again. Girls who abuse are more likely to engage in risky behavior that can lead to unwanted pregnancies and sexually transmitted diseases such as AIDS. They are more likely to be victims of domestic violence—beaten by husbands or boyfriends—as well as random violence on the street. In addition, in a world where women already have to work twice as hard to get half as far as men do, drugs can wreak havoc on women's sense of self-esteem, lessen their ambition, and lower their chances of success and happiness across the board. No matter what anyone tells you, remember that there's really no such thing as a happy drug addict.

Girl Power—Use It!

When it comes to drugs, it might seem as if everybody's telling you what to do. Your parents and teachers may tell you over and over again not to use drugs, that they are dangerous, and that you'll be punished if you take them. On the other hand, your friends or other kids you know may tell you just the opposite—that drugs are fun, exciting, or that they are essentially harmless.

On top of all that are the mixed messages you receive

from the media—certain rock stars singing the praises of various drugs while other celebrities die from an overdose, a drug-related accident, or drug-induced suicide. Fashion magazines push you to stay healthy with diet and exercise while simultaneously featuring models whose body types resemble that of a starving heroin addict. Even your parents may lecture you on the dangers of drugs while they themselves often indulge in an evening cocktail.

The point is that when it comes down to whether to smoke or not to smoke, to drink or not to drink, and so on, only you can decide whether or not you want to take that risk. Do you want to have control of your life? Do you want to make your own decisions? Then learn as much as you can about drugs and alcohol and their effects on you so that you can make an informed decision, because it's your body, your mind, and your life.

Veronica didn't smoke pot often, but she really liked it. She was just thirteen the first time she tried it with her best friend, Michelle, and Michelle's older sister, Nan. Veronica's parents were way strict—always watching her like a hawk—so she didn't get too many opportunities to light up. She smoked only once in a while, when Michelle's folks were out of the house after school and Nan was around with a supply of pot. It came down to no

more than once a month; she remained a first-string player on the basketball team, she kept her grades up, and she never got caught.

But when Veronica turned sixteen, things changed. Her parents let her *stay out later, and she got a part-time job. Suddenly she had some money to buy pot of her own and was able to go to the park after dark, where the local potheads liked to hang. Veronica found herself smoking every weekend, and soon she was doing it after school too.*

As time went by and Veronica continued smoking pot, she found it harder to concentrate on her schoolwork. The smoking was taking its toll on her health, and she found it hard to complete drills at practice. Her grades began to drop, and before long she was suspended from the basketball team. In addition, she'd stopped working out and was putting on weight. But somehow, she wasn't worried about it. She didn't seem to care.

Veronica got herself into some deep trouble. She thought that her drug of choice was harmless—after all, she'd been smoking pot for years without any adverse effects. But when she was suddenly able to smoke pot as often as she wanted, things changed pretty fast. Pot messes with short-term memory, strains the lungs, and makes users lazy and unambitious. Veronica, who was smart, athletic, and had a lot of great opportunities in front of her, was in danger of losing everything very quickly.

A Few Good Reasons

Every drug has some kind of effect on your body, mind, or both. Even drugs that seem harmless take their toll on you.

We'll talk about different types of drugs and how they affect your health and your life in the next chapter, but for now let's talk about some general truths. There are plenty of reasons to avoid abusing any and all substances. Here are a few of them.

Drugs Are Addictive

Most common drugs—alcohol, nicotine, cocaine, and others—are highly addictive. That means that once you start taking them, your body becomes dependent on them, and you need larger and larger doses in order to get high. And young people, whose bodies are growing and changing so quickly, can become physically addicted to drugs very fast. Just by trying something once or twice, a teen risks becoming painfully addicted. Take a look at your friends who smoke. Do you really want to spend all your time hiding in bathrooms at school, or missing the best parts of movies so that you can sneak off and smoke a butt?

Drugs Ruin Your Health

You've heard it before; now hear it again: Drugs are not good for you. Any kind of foreign substance that you put into your body—whether you smoke it, eat it, drink it, snort it, or shoot it—is going to take some toll on your body. Even things that are meant to improve your health, like medications, mess with your system. They may work to help your body in one way, but they almost always have some side effects that can hurt you if you're not careful. Why risk it at all?

Drugs Mess Up Your Mind

There's no doubt that drugs can screw up the way you think. Sedatives like alcohol and pot make you sleepy and cause countless car accidents every year. These and other drugs also impair your judgment, leading to risky behavior (including drunk driving, unprotected sex, and stupid contests like chicken).

But the effects of most drugs go even deeper. People who abuse often find that their short-term memory is shot—they're unable to keep basic facts straight even when they're sober. What's worse, addiction messes with your priorities and your judg-

ment—drugs become the single most important thing in an addict's life. Do you really want the most important thing in your life to be some stupid drug?

Drugs Affect Your Looks

In 1998 there was a lot of gossip running around that Courtney Love, the lead singer of the band Hole, had had mega plastic surgery. It wasn't that she looked like a different person, but she was suddenly looking great, when she used to look, well, kind of nasty—sickly and scrawny with big dark circles under her eyes all the time. In an interview on MTV, she told Kurt Loder that no, she hadn't had any surgery at all. "This is what happens," she said, "when you used to do drugs, and then you stop." Courtney—who had suffered from a horrific drug habit for years—had cleaned up her act, and she looked awesome because of it!

Anything that affects your health is going to affect your looks. Thinking about smoking? It's a fact that women who smoke age faster physically than women who don't. Smoking yellows the teeth and causes wrinkles. And more serious drugs have more serious effects on your looks. Alcohol abusers tend to put on weight, and they often suffer from burst blood vessels in the face, causing a ruddy and unhealthy-looking complexion. Abusers of diet drugs, heroin, and cocaine often lose so much weight that their breasts actually shrink, their complexion becomes ashy, and dark circles form beneath their eyes. Marijuana abuse brings on cravings for junk food, and abusers often adopt a lazy sort of lifestyle that frequently leads to weight gain.

Drugs Cost Money

Legal, illegal, or prescription, there's no way to avoid the fact that all drugs cost money. A pack-a-day smoking habit can wind up costing you more than twenty dollars per week. Illicit drugs cost even more. Users who become addicted may resort to stealing to keep up with their habit. And the health problems associated with drug use—even minor drug use—can cost an arm and a leg. When you think about it, it seems like the dumbest way to spend your cash.

The costs of drugs don't end there. Did you ever think about what it costs to get off of drugs once you are hooked? Dropping a serious drug habit, whether it's quitting smoking or detoxing from heroin, can be a long and painful process, and most people can't do it on their own. Their best shot at coming clean is through a drug treatment program, and like all forms of medical care, these programs often cost tons of money.

Drugs Spoil Your Chances

The statistics are simple: If you do drugs, you're less likely to achieve your dreams. Your chances of finishing high school or college decrease significantly if you abuse, and you increase your chances of ending up broke, in a lousy job, or in an unhappy relationship.

Drugs Hurt Those Around You

The real cost of abusing drugs far exceeds the money that users spend on them. Ask anyone who has lived with an

alcoholic or a drug addict, and you will hear countless stories of the ways he or she has been hurt—physically, mentally, emotionally—by someone else's addiction. And take a look at the way rampant drug abuse ruins schools, neighborhoods, and entire cities.

Do you want to be a mommy someday?

When it comes to drugs and alcohol, there's one thing women have to think about that men rarely do: the effect of substance abuse on the chances of bearing healthy children. As a female, you have the special ability to bring life into the world, an ability that carries special responsibilities. One of those responsibilities is to stay healthy and drug-free. Commonly abused drugs like nicotine, alcohol, opiates, and cocaine increase the risks of low birthweight and death in newborns. Many of them also cause serious birth defects. Some drugs, like pot, can inhibit your ability to have children. And women who are addicted are more likely to abuse or neglect their children than women who aren't. So if you've ever thought about being a mommy, you'd better think twice about drugs.

Drugs Cause Violence

In the home and on the street, drugs are the root cause of much of the violence that plagues our society. Women who abuse are more likely to be abused by the men in their lives; they are also more likely to beat or neglect their own children. And the trafficking of illegal drugs results in drug wars on the street, causing the deaths of not only dealers and users but countless innocent bystanders. And don't forget that the number one killer of young people in the United States is traffic accidents, most of which involve drugs, alcohol, or both.

Knowledge Is Power

Katie thought she had it all together. She was no fool. Her dad had just about killed himself drinking, and she had a friend whose brother had been shot by some dope dealer when he was walking to school. So she had made up her mind when she was just a little kid that she wasn't going to mess with any drugs. But then she was at this sleepover party at her friend Tonya's house when she was twelve, and she got high without even knowing what she was doing.

They had been hanging out, listening to music and goofing around on the Internet, when Tonya's cousin Christy crept into Tonya's brother's room and took a small bottle of glue meant for working on model airplanes. Christy plopped down on the sofa next to Katie, opened the bottle, and quickly sniffed deeply from the top. She started laughing hysterically and passed the bottle on to Katie, saying through her giggles, "Smell this." Without a thought, Katie smiled curiously and held the bottle up to her nose. She took a quick whiff, expecting to smell something funny or disgusting. But it just smelled sort of weird. Thinking she'd missed something, she took another, deeper sniff.

Katie suddenly felt dizzy, giddy, and strange. And she had no idea why. She jumped up from the couch quickly, wanting to walk over to Tonya and ask her what was going on. She lost her balance and tripped over the coffee table, hitting the floor face first. She wasn't hurt, but she had knocked a chip out of one of her front teeth.

Katie had made up her mind about drugs and alcohol but then found herself ambushed, using a drug pretty much by accident. Although the repercussions weren't all that severe, Katie was reminded of the stupid episode every time she looked in the mirror.

Why did it happen? Because Katie was uninformed. She'd never heard of getting high from sniffing glue. If she had known about this form of drug abuse, she would not have had to learn the hard way.

When it comes to alcohol, tobacco, and drugs, there's a lot a girl's got to know before she can stand tall and make a choice. Well, consider this book to be the dope on dope:

from cigarettes to sleeping pills, from pot to heroin. Because the more you know, the better equipped you'll be to make up your own mind.

Smoking

There are few people who don't know the dangers of smoking. Every pack of cigarettes sold and every cigarette advertisement by law must include warnings about the risks associated with smoking. Smoking causes cancer, lung disease, and heart disease; it clogs up arteries and weakens bones; and it causes wrinkles, ulcers, and cataracts. Tobacco is, in short, the number one killer drug in the United States.

Cigarettes (the most commonly abused form of tobacco) contain lots of nasty stuff, including tar—yes, the same tar they use to pave the street—and nicotine, a highly addictive drug. You shouldn't need a surgeon general's warning to tell you that putting that kind of junk into your lungs is not a good idea.

And people do know that smoking is bad for you—smoking on the whole is becoming less popular. But for some reason, teenage girls are one of the fastest growing groups of smokers. The number of female smokers between the ages of twelve and eighteen has doubled in the past twenty years, and teenage girls are now more likely to smoke than boys. Today 25 percent of all female deaths are smoking related.

Alcohol

Alcohol is another legal drug that is heavily abused. Like smoking, drinking is on the rise among women, and so is alcohol addiction (alcoholism). Today one out of three alcoholics in the United States is female.

Even though the girls may be drinking right alongside the boys, when it comes to alcohol, they're not really playing by the same rules. Girls are at a true disadvantage concerning alcohol. Studies show that women who abuse alcohol face even bigger health risks than men do, including an increased risk of liver damage, weakening of the immune system, and

even breast cancer. What's worse, recent research shows that women's bodies just can't break down and digest alcohol as well as men's do—that means they get drunk faster. And there's no nice way of saying it: When women get drunk, they tend to make stupid decisions. The fact that too much drinking can often lead to a really embarrassing pukefest is just the tip of the iceberg. A woman who is intoxicated is much more like-ly to engage in risky or even deadly behavior, such as driving drunk or having unwanted or unprotected sex.

Marijuana

Even though it is illegal, lots of kids smoke pot, which comes from the cannabis, or hemp, plant. It's a mood-altering drug that, if used often, can affect your state of mind even when you're not high. People who smoke pot frequently experience short-term memory loss and tend to become totally unambitious, unmotivated, and, well, lazy. What's more, smoking pot can lead to psychological addiction, resulting in depression. Add to that other health risks that mirror—even magnify—those of smoking: lung damage, sore throat, and endangering unborn children. And like alcohol, pot impairs your judgment and leads to many car accidents. Marijuana may seem harmless, but it's definitely not.

Inhalants

Abuse of inhalants by young people has also been on the rise in recent years. Why? Because they're easy for kids to get their hands on. Fumes from gasoline, model glue, some cleaning fluids, aerosol cans, and nitrous oxide cartridges (commonly called "whip-its") can bring on a kind of drunkenness if inhaled. Inhalants seem harmless, mainly because they are not controlled substances. But they are very dangerous—they can bring on hallucinations and even aggressiveness. And they are often flammable, so if you use them, you also risk having them burst into flames right in front of your face.

Diet Drugs

Many girls turn to diet drugs as a way to lose weight. Although these drugs are readily available in pharmacies and even supermarkets, that doesn't mean that they are safe to use. These drugs contain dangerous stimulants that have serious side effects, such as high blood pressure and anxiety attacks.

If you are concerned about being overweight, talk to your doctor. He or she can talk honestly with you about what to do. Many teen girls are worried about their weight when in fact they are normal and healthy. Instead of dieting, try starting up an exercise routine—biking, running, even stretching. Exercising helps keep your body in shape and your mind happy.

Cocaine and Crack

Cocaine is a powerful stimulant and is highly addictive. It is usually sold as a white powder that is snorted through the nose. It also comes in a crystal or rock form, commonly called crack, which is heated and smoked. Both can send your heart racing and cause heart attacks and heart failure even in healthy people.

Whereas cocaine is very expensive, crack is relatively cheap and very accessible to young people. What's worse, it's possible to become addicted to crack after only one hit. As with any highly addictive substance, the body tries to adapt to the effects of cocaine and crack, resulting in something called tolerance. This means that each time the drugs are used, the user must take more and more to get the same feeling. People who frequently abuse crack or cocaine can quickly find themselves needing to use all the time just to feel normal.

Opiates

Remember that scene from *The Wizard of Oz* where the wicked witch puts Dorothy and the gang to sleep in a field of poppies? That was a not-so-subtle reference to opiates, drugs that are derived from the flowers of the poppy plant. When it comes to drugs, not many are nastier than heroin, the most common opiate. Most heroin users shoot it into their veins with a hypodermic needle—a really disgusting thought, huh? Well, not only is it gross, but it's one of the most common ways people contract the AIDS virus.

These days there are forms of heroin that can be sniffed or smoked, which makes them danger-ously attractive to some teens. But don't let that fool you. Heroin is still one of the most addictive drugs out there, and addicts who try to quit face one of the most horrible and painful withdrawal processes there is.

Designer Drugs

Designer drugs are freaky things. They are made in illegal lab-oratories by amateur chemists who tinker with existing drugs to create new ones, which are usually more potent—and dan-gerous—than the original. One such drug, commonly called ecstasy, is very popular with teens and college students; it is a dangerous hallucinogen. Because they are not natural and are not made in controlled labs, designer drugs are very unpredictable. They are extremely powerful, and overdoses are common among users.

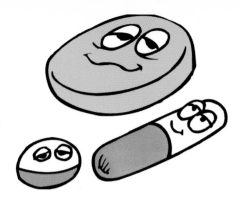

Uppers and Downers

Amphetamines—also known as uppers or speed—and barbiturates—commonly known as downers or sleeping pills—are prescription drugs that are widely abused. Uppers are stimulants; they keep users awake and produce a powerful high. They can be found not only as pills but also in crystal and powder forms. Users can come to depend on uppers to stay awake and on downers to calm them and put them to sleep. Both uppers and downers are extremely addictive and can be very dangerous if mixed with each other, with alcohol, or with other drugs. They are also very easy to overdose on, so if you don't want to end up like Marilyn Monroe—dead in the prime of her life from a sleeping pill overdose—don't go there!

Know the code!

Drugs come in many forms and are called by many names. It's good to be familiar with the street lingo when it comes to drugs so that you're well aware of what a substance is in case you find yourself in a situation where other kids are doing it, talking about it, or offering it to you. So here's a crash course in drug vocabulary, with the names of various drugs and their many forms.

Pot, dope, smoke, grass, mary jane, ganja, and kaya are all terms for marijuana; hashish or hash is another product of the cannabis plant that is a powerful drug.

A marijuana cigarette is often called a joint, spliff, or jay. Pot can also be smoked from a bong or a bowl (which is another word for a pipe).

Blow, snow, nose candy, and of course coke are all terms for powder cocaine; crack cocaine is sometimes referred to as rock.

Dope, smack, junk, and mud are slang words for heroin.

Uppers, or amphetamines, are also known as greenies, speed, meth, crank, crystal, ice, ups, black beauties, pep pills, benzedrine, or glass.

Downers include barbiturates and quaaludes.

Designer drugs include ecstasy, also known as X, XTC; synthetic heroin, or goodfella; and ketomine, known as special K, vitamin K, new ecstasy, or super-K.

Don't Go There!

4

On Marna's first day of high school, she met Keesha. Keesha seemed so incredibly cool—she knew all the older kids, wore awesome clothes, and had an air of confidence about her that made Marna want to be like her and be liked by her. When Keesha asked Marna if she wanted to hang out on a Friday night a few weeks after school started, Marna was psyched.

Keesha met Marna at the convenience store, and they headed out to a party at the house of a senior whose parents were away. As soon as they walked through the door, Marna was overwhelmed by the smells of pot and beer. She suddenly grew nervous: She had sworn to herself that she wouldn't mess with alcohol or drugs, at least not until she was a bit older. But she really wanted Keesha and all the other kids to like her.

As they moved through the room, Keesha worked the crowd, slapping hands and introducing Marna to other kids. When someone offered them each a toke on a joint, Marna froze. Before she had a chance to react, Keesha spoke up. *"Sorry, dude, we're not into that."*

They walked on through the party. "I hope you don't mind me answering for you," Keesha told Marna. "If you want some, go ahead and do it. We'll still hang out, but girl, if you're into that, I don't think we're ever gonna be really tight."

Being cool and doing drugs are not one and the same. Lots of kids—cool kids—don't use them and never have. Yet they hang out with other kids who do and don't let it bother them. Keesha is a natural leader, and it's a good thing Marna found her. She might have had a hard time saying no on her own.

There are many reasons why girls abuse. Fear of rejection, the need to fit in, and curiosity are some of them. But if you get it together, build your confidence, and find out the entire scoop on drugs and their effects, you'll be able to deal with all of those things no problem.

You've got the information. Now you have to make your own decision. Nobody else can make it for you—you've got to think for yourself on this one.

Free to Be Drug-Free

Once you've made a decision to refuse to use, you have to commit yourself to it. Remember that it's your decision, and trust yourself. Be proud of yourself. You've taken a great leap toward adulthood by coming to terms with the fact that you will have to deal with drugs at some point, and you'll be prepared when the time comes.

Making a commitment to a drug-free life is a very personal issue. Some girls may be vocal about their drug-free status, shouting it from the rooftops. They are very self-assured, and their confidence may inspire other girls to follow their

After living a life in the fast lane from a pretty young age, actress Drew Barrymore made the switch to a drug-free lifestyle and watched her career go through the roof!

Cool people who are drug-free

Seems as if all you hear about are rock stars dying of overdoses or singing the praises of various drugs. But some of the coolest musicians out there embrace a drug-free lifestyle; they sing instead of the dangers of drugs and the importance of spirituality and good health. Moby, The Mighty Mighty Bosstones, and Madonna all manage to rock without dipping into drugs. And even with bands that are closely associated with the drug culture, there are plenty of fans who dig the music and ditch the drugs. In fact, there are even organizations of drug-free concert goers who stick together at shows to dance without drugs!

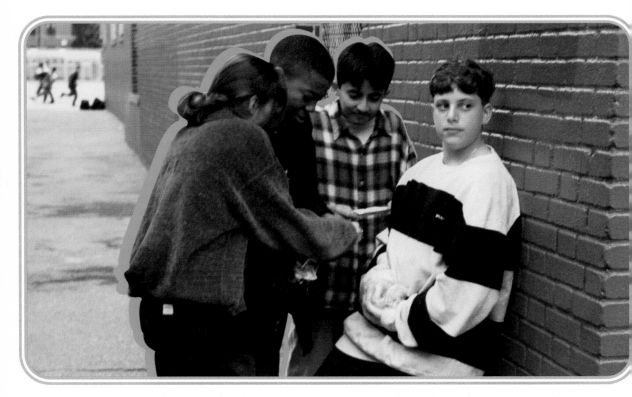

lead. For other girls their decision may be deeply personal, and their rejection of drugs and alcohol so understated that nobody even notices it.

A Girl's Gotta Do What a Girl's Gotta Do

Staying drug-free won't always be easy. Peer pressure is a very real thing. Everybody wants to be liked, to belong, and when you're a teenager, it sometimes feels as though nothing could be more important.

Your challenge is to keep a proper perspective on that desire to fit in. There will always be kids who will not take a simple no for an answer. When you feel pressure to do anything that you don't want to do, step back and ask yourself a few questions:

- ▶ *Do I want to do this?*

- ▶ *How much do I care if this person likes me or not?*

- ▶ *Is this person worth throwing away my own values for?*

- ▶ *Is this person going to like me less if I say no?*

- ▶ *Will this person respect me if I give in to his or her suggestions?*

- ▶ *Would I like someone less if he or she said no to me?*

You may find that the more you say no, the easier it becomes.

Standing Tall While Saying No

5

No doubt you've heard a lot about peer pressure. Anti-drug advocates sometimes make it sound as though saying no to drugs is terribly difficult, that your friends will try to pressure you into taking them, and that you'll have to change your life dramatically in order to stay drug-free. But listen up: Staying drug-free can be a very easy thing to do. You just have to be committed to yourself, confident in your decision, and prepared to deal with the consequences.

Let's say you're at a party and someone offers you a drink, a smoke, or some other drug. You can just say, "No, thanks" and chances are, whoever is offering it to you will leave it at that. Stay cool, and chances are that they will too. But if not, don't panic! There are many ways to say no.

Be Confident in Your Decision

When you say no, say it like you mean it without sounding as though it's a big deal. A simple "No, thanks" will usually do, tossed off as casually as if you were declining a cup of coffee. But if you are pressured further, stand firm. If you come off wimpy, you'll be treated that way.

Have a Reason Ready

Sometimes it helps to be prepared with a reason to back up your decision. Anything from "I don't like the taste of alcohol" to "I don't like being high" will show that you're not a chicken or blindly following the advice of your parents, but that you've thought about this and come to your own decision. Some teens use more detailed, personal reasons: "My mother

smokes three packs a day, and it totally grosses me out."
People have a hard time arguing with a good excuse.

Don't Be Judgmental

Remember that people who do drugs are bound to be sort
of defensive about it, and they may try to make themselves
feel better about their habit by making others feel worse
about theirs. So try to be fair. If you don't judge them harshly
for their decision to use drugs, they probably won't judge
you for refusing.

Pressure Them Back

If someone tries to pressure you, don't be afraid to argue
your point. Be tough, and nobody's gonna want to mess with
you! You might find that others are willing to follow your
lead—you could be the start of some positive peer pressure!

Make a Change

If you're feeling very pressured, don't be
afraid to leave the room, the party, or
the situation. Or try changing the sub-
ject. And don't be afraid to change
your friends if it comes to that. Do what-
ever you have to do to stay in control of
your life.

How to Stop Using

6

Marianna had a jar of booze in her backpack. It wasn't any particular kind of booze—it was a combination of any and every kind of liquor, taken a little bit at a time from her parents' liquor cabinet and from the houses of the people she baby-sat for. She called the precious potion her "special mix."

She'd been carrying the mix around for over a year now, taking from it and adding to it regularly. Her best friend, Sharon—her former best friend, that is—got all crazy when she found out that Marianna was carrying the jar around with her and drinking from it before school. Sharon was a big fake—she had started the mix with Marianna when they wanted to try getting drunk at a party about a year ago. But Marianna kept the mix going, and Sharon went nuts when Marianna started taking it to school, getting on a high horse and telling her that she was some sort of drunk. As if Sharon had never had a drink in her life. At school one day, she had accused Marianna of being an alcoholic. They hadn't spoken since.

If you, like Marianna, are using a drug in secret or at weird times of day, or are alienating friends and family over a drug, chances are that you've got a problem. You may have become addicted—the drug is making your decisions instead of you!

If You Want to Stop Using . . .

You don't have to be addicted to want to stop using drugs. Perhaps you are only an occasional user and are having second thoughts. Or maybe you didn't really give it enough thought when you started. A girl has a right to change her mind!

Just because you've used drugs already doesn't mean it's too late for you to change your mind and refuse to use.

Make the commitment now and stick to it. In fact, if you've been using drugs and don't want to anymore, you've got the perfect excuse to stop: Just tell folks you've tried them and don't like them!

. . . Or If You Think You Have a Problem

The first step toward solving your problem is to recognize that you have a problem. If you've already recognized this, then you're way ahead of the game. If not, ask yourself a few questions:

Have your friends been concerned about your use of substances?

Has your drug or alcohol use caused problems for you at school?

Do you use drugs early in the morning, before or during school, or to prepare for situations that might be difficult?

When something bothers you, do you choose to get drunk or high instead of dealing with it?

Have you been developing a tolerance to drugs or alcohol, meaning that you have to use more and more to get the same effect?

Have you hurt yourself or anyone else while you were drunk or high?

Do you ever feel guilty about your drinking or drug use?

Have you found it difficult not to use drugs or alcohol?

Have you experienced any weird reactions—physical or mental—when you've stopped using drugs or alcohol?

If you've answered yes to any of these questions, you may have a problem. But don't worry—you can fix it! Talk to your friends, teachers, or parents, or call one of the drug or alcohol hotlines listed at the end of this book. If you take the first step on your own, you're already halfway there!

You Are Your Sister's Keeper!

If you've got a friend who is using or even addicted, you have a responsibility to try to help her. And that does not mean covering for her when she's screwing up at school or in trouble with her parents. In fact, if you're lying to anyone to hide your friend's drug use, you are contributing to her problem!

The truth is, when it comes to drugs, girls have to stick together. If you have friends who are using, let them know that you think they are making a mistake and that you don't want any part of it. Don't be judgmental, but make your point clear. (Use the tips from the previous chapter to help you.) And tell them you'd expect the same courtesy from them if you were doing something dangerous and unhealthy.

And if you think your friend has an addiction, be tough. You aren't going to be any use to her if you just watch her throw her life away. Find out where she can get help, and offer to go along with her. Just put yourself in her shoes and think how you'd want to be treated if you had this problem. And let her know that you'll stick by her!

Of course, she may not want your help. Most people have a hard time recognizing their own problems and will blow off any offers of help. If this happens, don't be afraid to pull back and pull out. Just tell her that you'll be there for her if she ever changes her mind. And take care of yourself!

Inspiration from folks who've been there:

When it comes to dealing with an addiction, there's strength in numbers. Joining a support group like Alcoholics or Narcotics Anonymous can help you to create a network of girls who've been there and who can relate to your problem. You can find local groups listed right in the Yellow Pages, or turn to the listings at the end of this book.

Find Your Own High!

7

Take a look at some of the key reasons why teens do drugs: They're bored. They're curious. They're adventurous. They're trying to find ways to express themselves. Well, there are plenty of great ways to deal with boredom, express yourself, and satisfy your own curiosity and craving for excitement and adventure without using drugs.

Read All About It

Curious? Go down to your local library and read all about the ups and downs of drug use and abuse. There are many real stories of people you might respect or relate to who have battled drug use. Some, like Kurt Cobain, Janis Joplin, and actor River Phoenix, lost. Others, like members of the rock group Aerosmith and actress Drew Barrymore, have won the battle and embraced their new, sober lifestyle. Reading their stories can satisfy your curiosity while reaffirming your decision to refuse to use!

Express yourself!

Got something to say? Explore the arts! Dancing, acting, painting, and writing are all great outlets for your creative energy and the stress and confusion of your teenage years. Venting all of your anger, fear, curiosity, and excitement on a canvas, dance floor, stage, or page can be very therapeutic and can create great art in the process!

Join the Club!

Boredom is a key factor in teen drug use. Keeping busy is important to avoid being sucked in, and joining a club is a great way to avoid boredom and build self-esteem, one of the biggest keys to being a strong woman. Take a look at what's going on in your school or town, and think about how you might want to spend your time. Check out the school newspaper, band, chess club, and choir, as well as athletic teams.

Get in Shape, Girl!

There's nothing wrong with getting in shape, and girls who keep fit are less likely to get involved with drugs. After all, who'd want to put that much work into a hot bod only to ruin it with nasty stuff? Joining school teams or intramural athletic leagues is great for building confidence and self-esteem as well as for getting in shape. But your sport doesn't have to be a competitive or team-oriented thing. Think about karate, yoga, or running—all great ways to keep fit and get in tune with your body and mind!

Have Fun!

When you're at a party, a dance, or just out with friends, don't be afraid to let loose and have fun. You don't need drugs to dance, to talk to boys, or to enjoy yourself. In fact, you might find that you can have more fun than your friends who do use drugs, because you'll be in control of yourself and won't have to worry about feeling foolish the next day!

Stick Together!

When it comes to staying drug-free, nothing works better than a support group. As you grow up, you'll find that some of your friends will turn to drugs, and you'll also meet new friends who have chosen not to. By surrounding yourself with a network of drug-free friends, you'll always have someone to stand by you.

abuse   To put to a wrong or improper use.

addiction   The compulsive need for and use of a habit-forming substance; the persistent use of a substance known by the user to be harmful.

AIDS (acquired immune deficiency syndrome)   A chronic disease caused by the HIV virus that debilitates the immune system, making even the simplest infections life-threatening.

detox   The process of freeing a person from a dependence on a certain substance.

domestic violence   Physical abuse that occurs in the home, usually perpetrated by a husband on a wife.

hallucinations   Seeing or hearing things that are not real as a result of a disorder in the nervous system or in response to certain drugs.

hypodermic   Beneath the skin; refers to injection with a needle.

prescription   A drug that can be obtained only with the written permission of a doctor.

sedatives   The class of drugs including alcohol and sleeping pills that lowers a person's heart rate; these drugs are addictive and can be fatal if taken incorrectly or mixed with each other.

self-esteem   Confidence in and satisfaction with oneself.

stimulants   The class of drugs including cocaine and amphetamines, that increases a person's heart rate; they are addictive and can be fatal.

tolerance   The body's natural capacity to endure or become less responsive to a chemical substance.

vent   To release feelings of anger and frustration in order to move beyond negative feelings and deal with a problem calmly.

It's a Girl's World
It's a Girl's World
It's a Girl's World
It's a

It's a Girl's World:
helpful info

Drug Abuse Resistance Education (DARE)
Web site: http://www.dare-america.com
Drug awareness program run by police officers that teaches kids how to deal with drugs and violence in their schools and neighborhoods.

The Partnership for a Drug-Free America (PDFA)
405 Lexington Avenue
New York, NY 10174
Web site: http://www.drugfreeamerica.org
Provides accurate information on drug abuse and addiction.

The Smoke-Free Class of 2000
Web site: http://www.tiedrich.com/clients/smokefree
A smoking awareness project with a great Web site, written by and for kids.

Students Against Destructive Decisions (SADD)
Web site: http://www.saddonline.com
Students dedicated to helping students make smart decisions concerning drinking, drugs, and safe driving.

The Women's Addiction Foundation
B.C. Women's Hospital
4500 Oak Street, E500B
Vancouver, BC V6H 3N1
(604) 875-3756
Web site: http://www.womenfdn.org
Canadian foundation that offers support, advice, and help to women who have become addicted to alcohol or other drugs.

Aerosmith and Stephen Davis. *Walk This Way: The Autobiography of Aerosmith*. New York: Avon Books, 1997.

Anonymous and James Jennings. *Go Ask Alice*. New York: Simon & Schuster, 1998.

Barrymore, Drew, and Todd Gold. *Little Girl Lost: A Child Star's Descent into Addiction—and Out Again*. New York: Pocket Books, 1991.

The Boston Women's Health Book Collective. *The New Our Bodies, Ourselves: A Book by and for Women*. New York: Touchstone, 1992.

Carlson, Karen J., et al. *The Harvard Guide to Women's Health*. Cambridge, MA: The President and Fellows of Harvard College, 1992.

Glass, George. *Drugs and Fitting In*. New York: Rosen Publishing Group, 1998.

Klein, Wendy. *Drugs and Denial*. New York: Rosen Publishing Group, 1998.

Queen Latifah and Karen Hunter. *Ladies First: Revelations from a Strong Woman*. New York: William Morrow & Co., 1999.

Ryan, Elizabeth A. *Straight Talk About Drugs and Alcohol*. New York: Facts on File, 1995.

Index

Credits

About the Author

Ann Kirby-Payne is a writer and editor who lives in Rockaway Beach, New York. A graduate of the State University of New York, The College at New Paltz, she covered drug and alcohol abuse policy while interning as a journalist at the state capitol in 1991.

Photo Credits

Cover photo by Brian Silak; pp. 6, 11, 15 by John Bentham; p. 9 by Ethan Zindler; p. 18 by Lauren Piperno; p. 20 by Pablo Maldonado; p. 21 © Archme Photos; pp. 22, 30, 36 by Seth Dinnerman; pp. 23, 38 by John Nova; pp. 25, 33 by Ira Fox; p. 29 © The Everett Collection; p. 37 by Sarah Friedman; p. 41 by Ryan Giuliani.

Series Design

Laura Murawski

Layout

Oliver Rosenberg